DISCOVERING TIGERS, LIONS & OTHER BIG CATS

by Kelly Gauthier

Illustrated by Julius Csotonyi

APPLESAUCE PRESS

KENNEBUNKPORT, MAINE

TABLE OF CONTENTS

INTRODUCTION

Have you ever wondered why a pet kitten is content to cuddle on the couch instead of adventuring through the forest? It's because house cats are a domestic species, *Felis catus*, that is part of a family of animals called Felidae. There are nearly 40 different species in the Felidae family, and only one of those species—the domestic cat—is meant to live indoors alongside people. The rest of the cat species are wild animals that can be found all over the world.

Cats (even the domestic ones) are carnivores, and they have claws and teeth that allow them to hunt efficiently. Many cats prefer to hunt alone, and a lot of them are nocturnal. They use a method of hunting where they stalk and ambush their prey. If you're trying to picture what that looks like, think about how house cats play with toys that look like mice or birds on a string. You might make the toy move and wiggle, and the cat will usually slink down low, wait for the perfect moment, and then pounce to snatch it.

The Felidae family has two main groups: the Felinae subfamily and the Panthera subfamily. The Felinae subfamily has a lot more species in it than the Panthera subfamily does—the biggest difference between the two is whether the cat purrs or roars. Purring cats all belong to the Felinae subfamily, and roaring cats all belong to the Panthera subfamily. Roaring cats are the ones you might think of as "big cats." Tigers, lions, leopards, and jaguars are the only species of cat that can roar, so they're the only ones that are part of the Panthera subfamily. The rest of the wild cat species purr and fall into the Felinae subfamily.

All cats have a few things in common. Their front paws have five toes (usually four near the ground and a dewclaw higher up) and their back paws have four toes. Their claws are retractile, which means that the claws can be exposed or pulled back into the toes. Some cats can fully pull their claws in and out, while others can only partially retract their claws. Cats all have large canine teeth and excellent night vision. If you've ever been licked by a cat, you know that its tongue has a really strange texture. Cat tongues are covered in structures called papillae that help them both eat meat and groom. And all cats have whiskers that help them navigate in the dark and sense prey.

Even though there are similarities between species, each cat is unique in their coloring, habitat, size, and behavior. So let's jump right in and discover more about cats!

CHAPTER 1

ANCIENT CATS AND ALMOST-CATS

Ancestors of cats and catlike creatures have been around since prehistoric times. Some of these creatures went extinct over time, some evolved into other types of mammals, and some eventually became the group we know today as cats. Scientists learned what these prehistoric creatures looked like and where they lived through the study of their fossils. And while you might think big cats today look intimidating, the cats of prehistoric times were even bigger and scarier, like the massive Ngandong tiger, the widespread marsupial lion, and the terrifying saber-toothed cat.

Today, there are lots of animals that evolved from similar ancient ancestors. They're not quite cats, but they have lots of similar traits. In this chapter, we'll look at both the ancient creatures that paved the way for modern cats and their current relatives that share similar traits.

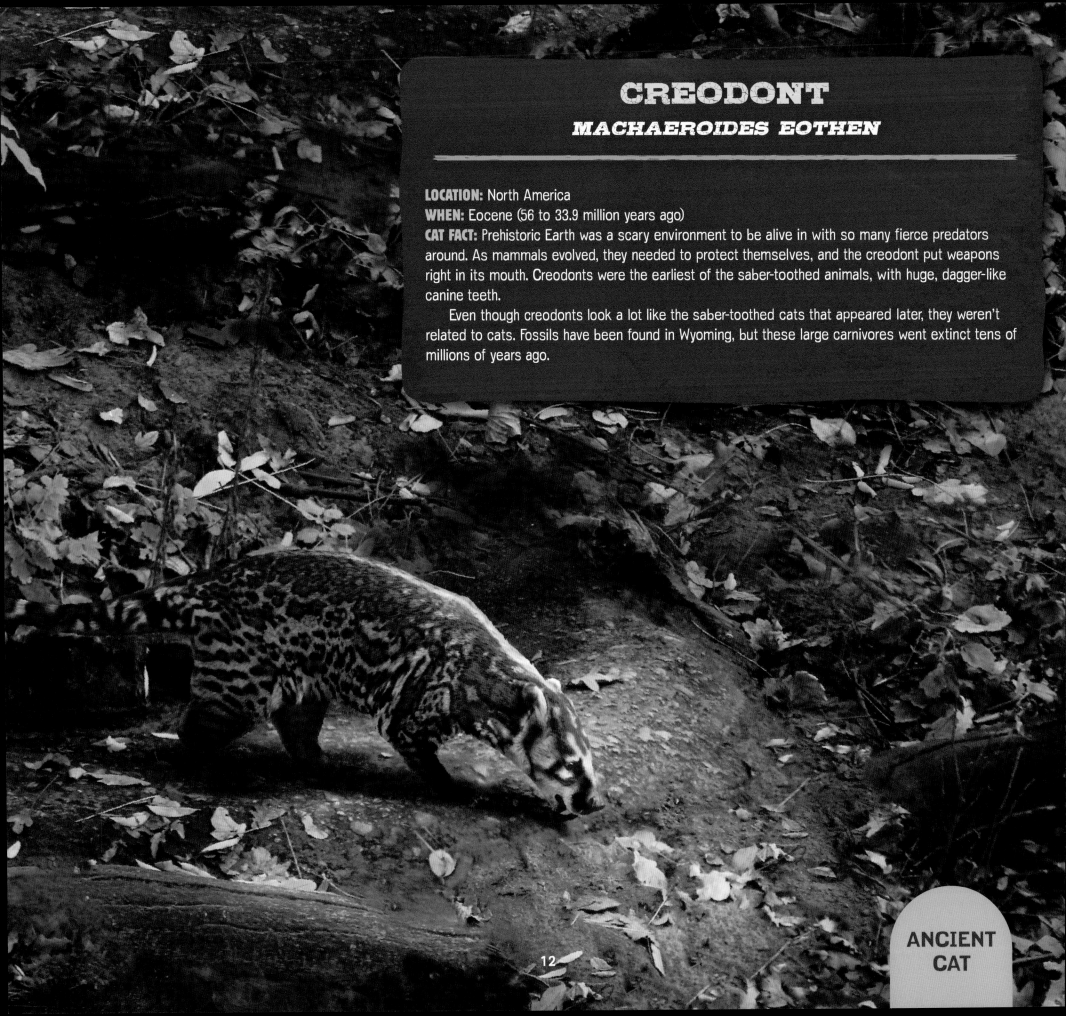

CREODONT
MACHAEROIDES EOTHEN

LOCATION: North America

WHEN: Eocene (56 to 33.9 million years ago)

CAT FACT: Prehistoric Earth was a scary environment to be alive in with so many fierce predators around. As mammals evolved, they needed to protect themselves, and the creodont put weapons right in its mouth. Creodonts were the earliest of the saber-toothed animals, with huge, dagger-like canine teeth.

Even though creodonts look a lot like the saber-toothed cats that appeared later, they weren't related to cats. Fossils have been found in Wyoming, but these large carnivores went extinct tens of millions of years ago.

ANCIENT CAT

EARLY SABER-TOOTHED SPARASSODONT

EOMAKHAIRA MOLOSSUS

LOCATION: South America

WHEN: Oligocene (33.9 to 23 million years ago)

CAT FACT: Extra, extra! The early saber-toothed sparassodont is breaking news in the science world. The first reports of this species started popping up in 2020, so scientists still have a lot to learn about this creature. The sparassodonts were a prehistoric order of carnivorous mammals in South America. This early saber-tooth had long, curved canines that later became a trademark of prehistoric catlike predators.

SABER-TOOTHED SPARASSODONT

PATAGOSMILUS GOINI

LOCATION: South America

WHEN: Miocene (23 to 5.3 million years ago)

CAT FACT: Get a look at those fangs! Next up in the timeline of non-cat saber-tooths is this sparassodont. Remnants of its skull were found in Patagonia, Argentina. The name *Patagosmilus* actually means Patagonian knife—no doubt a reference to those long, dagger-like teeth. When different species develop the same traits, it's called convergent evolution. That's what happened with the sparassodont. It evolved with the same long canine teeth as the saber-toothed cat because they were useful at the time, but as it continued to evolve it changed again. The sparassodont ended up more closely related to the modern marsupial than to cats.

14

ANCIENT
CAT

SUPER-SABER-TOOTHED SPARASSODONT
THYLACOSMILUS ATROX

LOCATION: South America
WHEN: Miocene and Pliocene (23 to 2.4 million years ago)
CAT FACT: Teeth that big would have to be pretty heavy, and that may have been why this sparassodont had such a big jaw. The large jaw would have served as support and protection for the sparassodont's claw-like teeth when its mouth was closed. The massive teeth were actually continuously growing, so if they wore down they would just grow larger again. The teeth alone could grow to around 7 inches long, and the rest of the super-saber-tooth was likely about the size of a modern leopard. Like other sparassodonts, this one isn't related to big cats; it's more closely related to modern marsupials.

15

ANCIENT CAT

MARSUPIAL LION
THYLACOLEO CARNIFEX

LOCATION: Australia

WHEN: Pleistocene (2.58 million to 11,700 years ago)

CAT FACT: Imagine being the only meat-eater in a family of vegetarians! You might feel a little out of place at the dinner table if nobody else liked to eat what you did. That's what happened with the marsupial lion. The rest of the members in its family line were all herbivores, but the marsupial lion had large, serrated teeth that tell scientists it probably ate meat. None of its modern relatives eat meat, though—that branch of mammals led to modern herbivorous marsupials like koalas and kangaroos.

SABER-TOOTHED NIMRAVID

HOPLOPHONEUS MENTALIS

LOCATION: North America

WHEN: Late Eocene and Early Oligocene (38 to 23 million years ago)

CAT FACT: I know what you're thinking—the nimravid looks an awful lot like a big cat...but even though it looks like the modern leopard, the nimravid wasn't quite a cat. It had the saber-like teeth of a carnivore and a stocky build with short legs, but it had a different bone structure than the line that led to modern big cats.

ANCIENT CAT

17

TRUE SABER NIMRAVID
EUSMILUS BIDENTATUS

LOCATION: Europe

WHEN: Late Eocene and Early Oligocene (38 to 23 million years ago)

CAT FACT: Do you know what a doppelgänger is? It's someone who looks just like another person even though they aren't related. That's kind of what the nimravid is: a doppelgänger of the actual saber-toothed cat. They look so similar that nimravids are even sometimes called "false saber-toothed cats."

Nimravids were fierce predators. Their jaws weren't incredibly strong, so they didn't really bite their prey by closing their mouths. Instead, their shoulders and necks were super strong, so they would slam their whole head, saber-teeth included, down on their prey in a quick killing blow.

SABER-TOOTHED FELIFORM
BARBOUROFELIS FRICKI

LOCATION: North America

WHEN: Miocene (23 to 5.3 million years ago)

CAT FACT: Take a look at the modern lion and you'll see just how huge the feliform was. It would have been similar in size to a lion with its bulky body, though it probably walked a little more like a bear. It had large saber-like teeth, and it was the last in the line of nimravids, so it was not a true cat. It had a big lower jaw to help support the weight of its teeth when its mouth was closed.

ANCIENT CAT

SCIMITAR-TOOTHED CAT
HOMOTHERIUM SERUM

LOCATION: North America

WHEN: Pliocene and Pleistocene (5.4 million to 11,700 years ago)

CAT FACT: Lots of prehistoric creatures were called saber-toothed because their teeth looked like sabers, but this cat was named for a different type of sword. A scimitar is a short sword that has a curved blade and a broad point. No matter what kind of sword they're named after, it's safe to say those pointed teeth were pretty intimidating.

The scimitar-toothed cat was part of a family of animals called Felidae, which also contained the saber-toothed cat and eventually led to modern cat species. The scimitar-toothed cat would have been fairly quick and agile, and likely could have pursued its prey for a while before getting tired.

SABER-TOOTHED CAT
SMILODON FATALIS

LOCATION: North and South America

WHEN: Pleistocene (2.58 million to 11,700 years ago)

CAT FACT: It's one of the most famous prehistoric mammals for a reason; few ancient creatures were more fearsome than the saber-toothed cat. It was an apex predator, which means it was at the top of the food chain, and it hunted huge herbivores like ancient bison. The saber-tooth could weigh up to 600 pounds, and it was as large as modern tigers. Its teeth were long, flat, and pointed to easily pierce through prey. Modern cats can open their jaws about 65 degrees wide, but saber-tooths could open their enormous mouths 130 degrees to take a huge bite! They were part of the Felidae family that eventually evolved into cats, so they're distantly related to modern cats.

ANCIENT CAT

AMERICAN LION
PANTHERA ATROX

LOCATION: North America

WHEN: Pleistocene and Early Holocene (2.58 million to 8,000 years ago)

CAT FACT: Have you ever wondered what your neighborhood looked like tens of thousands of years ago? Nowadays, humans are the mammals that cover most of the Earth, but back in its day the American lion was one of the most widespread mammals and top of the food chain. They covered the land all the way from Canada to Mexico, and there was a similar species in Africa. The American lion looked a lot like a modern lion without the mane, but its body was even bigger and heavier!

22

ANCIENT
CAT

23

NGANDONG TIGER

PANTHERA TIGRIS SOLOENSIS

LOCATION: Southeastern Asia

WHEN: Pleistocene (2.58 million to 11,700 years ago)

CAT FACT: When scientists find fossils of prehistoric creatures, they can't always put together a skeleton of their whole bodies. Sometimes they only find certain body parts, and when that happens they have to make smart guesses about what the animal would have looked and acted like. So far, scientists have only found 7 fossils of the Ngandong tiger, so there's still a lot for them to learn. All the fossils were found in the same area, and from what they do know, scientists think it was probably at least as big as the American lion or saber-toothed cat. But some scientists think it could have been even larger—maybe even as long as 13 feet from head to tail and as heavy as 1,000 pounds. If those estimates are true, then the Ngangdong tiger would have been the biggest cat to ever exist!

ANCIENT CAT

NATIVE CAT
DASYURUS MACULATUS

LOCATION: Australia

AVERAGE SIZE: 2.5 to 3 feet (0.75 to 0.9 meters) long

CAT FACT: Sometimes the native cat is chased by the devil…the Tasmanian devil, that is. Both the native cat and the Tasmanian devil are carnivorous marsupials, just like the marsupial lion was. Marsupials are mammals that carry their young in pouches, and even though they're not cats they are related to ancient catlike creatures.

The native cat is also called the tiger quoll or the spotted-tail quoll, and it will eat just about anything from insects, lizards, snakes, and birds to platypus, rabbits, possums, wallabies, and wombats. But the Tasmanian devil is a lot more intimidating than the native cat, and the devil will often steal the native cat's kill.

MODERN ALMOST-CAT

AFRICAN PALM CIVET
NANDINIA BINOTATA

LOCATION: Africa
AVERAGE SIZE: 1.5 to 2 feet (0.45 to 0.6 meters) long
CAT FACT: African palm civets know how to throw dinner parties. They usually like to be on their own, but when there's a lot of food available they'll gather in groups of up to 15 civets to eat. Civets are part of a group of carnivorous mammals called feliforms. That group includes true cats as well as creatures that aren't true cats but are still catlike.

African palm civets are omnivores, which means they eat both plants and animals. They enjoy fruits as well as small rodents, lizards, and birds.

MODERN
ALMOST-
CAT

27

FOSSA
CRYPTOPROCTA FEROX

LOCATION: Madagascar

AVERAGE SIZE: 2 feet (0.6 meters) long, plus a 2-foot-long tail

CAT FACT: The fossa is a modern example of convergent evolution. Even though the fossa isn't a cat, it has developed a lot of catlike features that make it look like a small cougar. It's able to climb well because of its semi-retractable claws, and it can jump from tree to tree. But it's more closely related to mongooses than it is to cats.

28

MODERN ALMOST-CAT

FANALOKA
FOSSA FOSSANA

LOCATION: Madagascar
AVERAGE SIZE: 1.5 feet (0.45 meters) long
CAT FACT: If you took the face of a fox and put it on the body of a house cat, you would end up with something that looks like the fanaloka. Its brown body has dark spots and stripes, and it has a short but thick tail. The fanaloka is a civet, and like the African palm civet it's part of the feliform group of catlike creatures.

The secretive fanaloka is a great thief. It will steal eggs to eat right out of birds' nests. It will also eat insects, aquatic animals, and other small creatures.

BANDED LINSANG
PRIONODON LINSANG

LOCATION: Southeast Asia

AVERAGE SIZE: About 1.5 feet (0.45 meters) long, plus a 1-foot-long tail (0.3 meters)

CAT FACT: Imagine a mammal that moves like a snake. The banded linsang practically slithers when it hunts, keeping its body low to the ground and stalking its prey like a snake does. The dark bands on its fur act as camouflage so it blends into the ground.

Linsangs are tree-dwelling, carnivorous mammals that aren't quite cats; they're part of a similar group of animals called prionodons that are very close relatives to cats.

SPOTTED LINSANG
PRIONODON PARDICOLOR

LOCATION: Southeast Asia

AVERAGE SIZE: About 1.5 feet (0.45 meters) long, plus a 1-foot-long tail (0.3 meters)

CAT FACT: The spotted linsang is part of the same family as the banded form, and the biggest difference between the two is the markings on their velvety fur. You might have already guessed it, but the spotted linsang has spots.

The spotted linsang spends most of its time in trees, and it has a thin body and sharp claws that help it easily run along branches.

33

CHAPTER 2

SOVEREIGNS OF THE SAVANNA

Savannas are unique environments of grassy plains where the trees are spread far apart and there's lots of open space. But open space means that there's nowhere to hide, and some of the biggest, baddest predatory cats call the savannas home. Have you ever heard the phrase "king of the jungle"? Big cats are the apex predators in savannas with their incredible size and speed, like the huge East African lion or the swift North African cheetah. In this chapter, we'll look at the cats that rule the savanna.

EAST AFRICAN LION
PANTHERA LEO MELANOCHAITA

LOCATION: Southern and East Africa

AVERAGE SIZE: About 8 to 9 feet (2.4 to 2.75 meters) long

CAT FACT: A lion's mane is probably its most recognizable feature, but you might not have known that the manes can be different colors—just like how people can have different hair colors! Male East African lions have black manes that make them look bigger and more intimidating. Lions are the only big cats with tufts on their tails, and those black tufts might be used to communicate with other lions on the hunt or to get cubs to follow female lions.

The East African lion might look big, but it can still sneak up on its prey pretty easily. It eats large prey including antelopes, gazelles, warthogs, zebras, buffalo, giraffes, and young elephants. It has retractable claws and walks on its toes so it's super quiet while hunting. But when predators like other lions or hyenas are approaching, it doesn't want to be quiet; when it's trying to be scary it wants to be loud. Lions have the loudest roar of all big cats, and it can be heard from 5 miles away!

CARACAL
CARACAL CARACAL

LOCATION: Africa and Central and Southwestern Asia
AVERAGE SIZE: About 3 to 4 feet (0.9 to 1.2 meters) long
CAT FACT: Have you ever seen a cat use a scratching post? It's not just something house cats do; the caracal uses trees like scratching posts to sharpen its claws. Having them sharp is important since it climbs trees. Sometimes it will even bring its prey up into the branches to save for later—usually it eats rodents, birds, or small monkeys, but sometimes it will take on larger prey like antelopes or gazelles.

Its trademark is its long ears with black tufts, and it will twitch the tufts to communicate with other caracals.

NORTHWEST AFRICAN CHEETAH
ACINONYX JUBATUS HECKI

LOCATION: Northwest Africa

AVERAGE SIZE: About 4 feet (1.2 meters) long, plus a 2- to 3-foot-long tail (0.6 to 0.9 meters)

CAT FACT: Imagine living in the middle of the desert, where the temperature is easily well over 100 degrees Fahrenheit during the day and there's little to no rain. It might not sound like a great place to live to you, but for these cheetahs it's home.

Cheetahs have recognizable spots down their back that fade from black to brown, and they have white bellies and white spots around their eyes. Take a look at their hind feet and you'll notice there aren't any spots there. They're superfast runners, and they hunt gazelles, zebras, and ostriches.

AFRICAN SAVANNA LEOPARD
PANTHERA PARDUS PARDUS

LOCATION: Africa

AVERAGE SIZE: 5 to 7 feet (1.5 to 2 meters) long

CAT FACT: Did you know that humans can only survive 3 days without water? The African savanna leopard can go triple that amount of time. It can last up to 10 days without anything to drink. That gives it plenty of time to focus on hunting, and it will eat anything from rodents and birds to young giraffes. But its favorite prey is the impala, a type of antelope found in eastern and southern Africa.

Leopards are recognizable because of their spots, but those spots are actually a pattern called rosettes. Rosettes are a collection of a few spots in a circle, kind of like a rose. The African savanna leopard is the largest of all the different species of leopards.

CHAPTER 3

FELINES OF THE FOREST

There are lots of dangerous things living in forests, and for smaller forest-dwelling cats, trees and branches can be an important source of protection. They can hide among the branches to rest and bring their prey up into the trees to keep it safe from bigger predators. But some of the most dangerous creatures in the forest are the big cats living there, like the jaguars and leopards that prowl among the trees to stay hidden while they hunt down their prey. In this chapter, we'll look at the different types of cats, big and small, that call the forest their home.

AFRICAN GOLDEN CAT
CARACAL AURATA

LOCATION: Africa

AVERAGE SIZE: About 2 to 3 feet (0.6 to 0.9 meters) long, plus a 1-foot-long tail (0.3 meters)

CAT FACT: When you're related to someone, like an aunt or a cousin, you might look similar to them, but not exactly the same. That happens with animals, too. Species that are closely related will look similar to each other, but not exactly the same. That's the case for the two subspecies of African golden cats. They aren't actually golden—they have brown, reddish, or grayish fur, but while the *Caracal aurata aurata* has a plain coat, the *Caracal aurata celidogaster* is spotted.

Both species like tropical forests and eat birds, rodents, monkeys, hogs, and antelopes. And both have white patches around their eyes and on their cheeks. Just look for the spots to tell the two apart!

ASIAN GOLDEN CAT
CATOPUMA TEMMINCKII

LOCATION: Southeast Asia, Northeast India, and Southern China

AVERAGE SIZE: About 4 to 5 feet (1.2 to 1.5 meters) long

CAT FACT: House cats have a habit of rubbing their heads up against things (like your legs, or a favorite toy). They leave their unique scent as a way of marking the location or object. Asian golden cats do the same, rubbing their heads up against trees to mark them with their scent. This communicates to other cats that they're there without them ever having to make any noise.

Their fur can be golden like their name suggests, but it can also be darker brown or even reddish, and they have white and black lines on top of their head, around their eyes, and down their necks.

45

SOUTH AMERICAN OCELOT

LEOPARDUS PARDALIS MITIS

LOCATION: South America

AVERAGE SIZE: About 2 to 3 feet (0.6 to 0.9 meters) long, plus a 1-foot-long tail (0.3 meters)

CAT FACT: If you were going out into the woods and didn't want to be seen, you might wear camouflage clothing. The ocelot's fur is its very own camouflage! It has a golden color with dark gray splotches and stripes that help it blend into its surroundings while it hunts on the ground for rodents, reptiles, armadillos, and deer. And it doesn't just stay on the ground—ocelots are great swimmers and climbers, too.

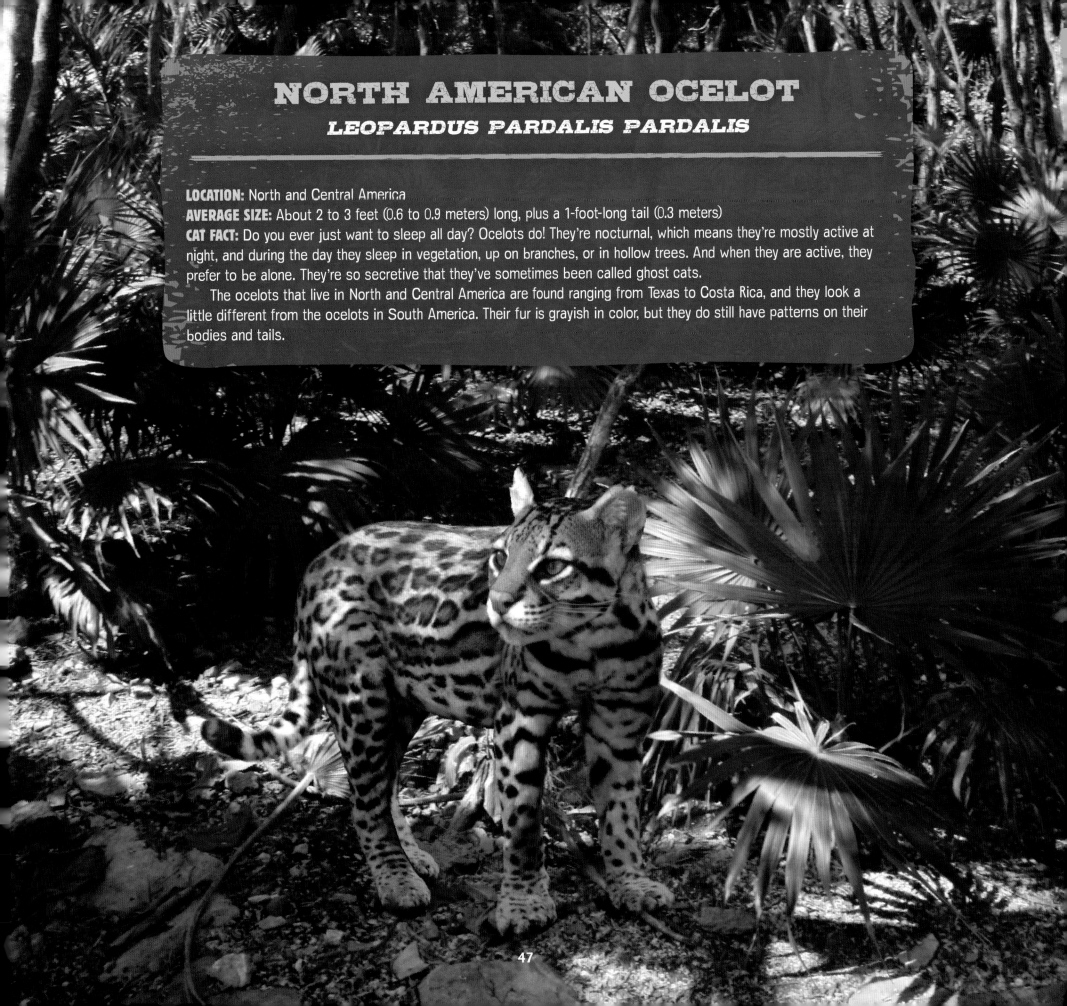

NORTH AMERICAN OCELOT
LEOPARDUS PARDALIS PARDALIS

LOCATION: North and Central America

AVERAGE SIZE: About 2 to 3 feet (0.6 to 0.9 meters) long, plus a 1-foot-long tail (0.3 meters)

CAT FACT: Do you ever just want to sleep all day? Ocelots do! They're nocturnal, which means they're mostly active at night, and during the day they sleep in vegetation, up on branches, or in hollow trees. And when they are active, they prefer to be alone. They're so secretive that they've sometimes been called ghost cats.

The ocelots that live in North and Central America are found ranging from Texas to Costa Rica, and they look a little different from the ocelots in South America. Their fur is grayish in color, but they do still have patterns on their bodies and tails.

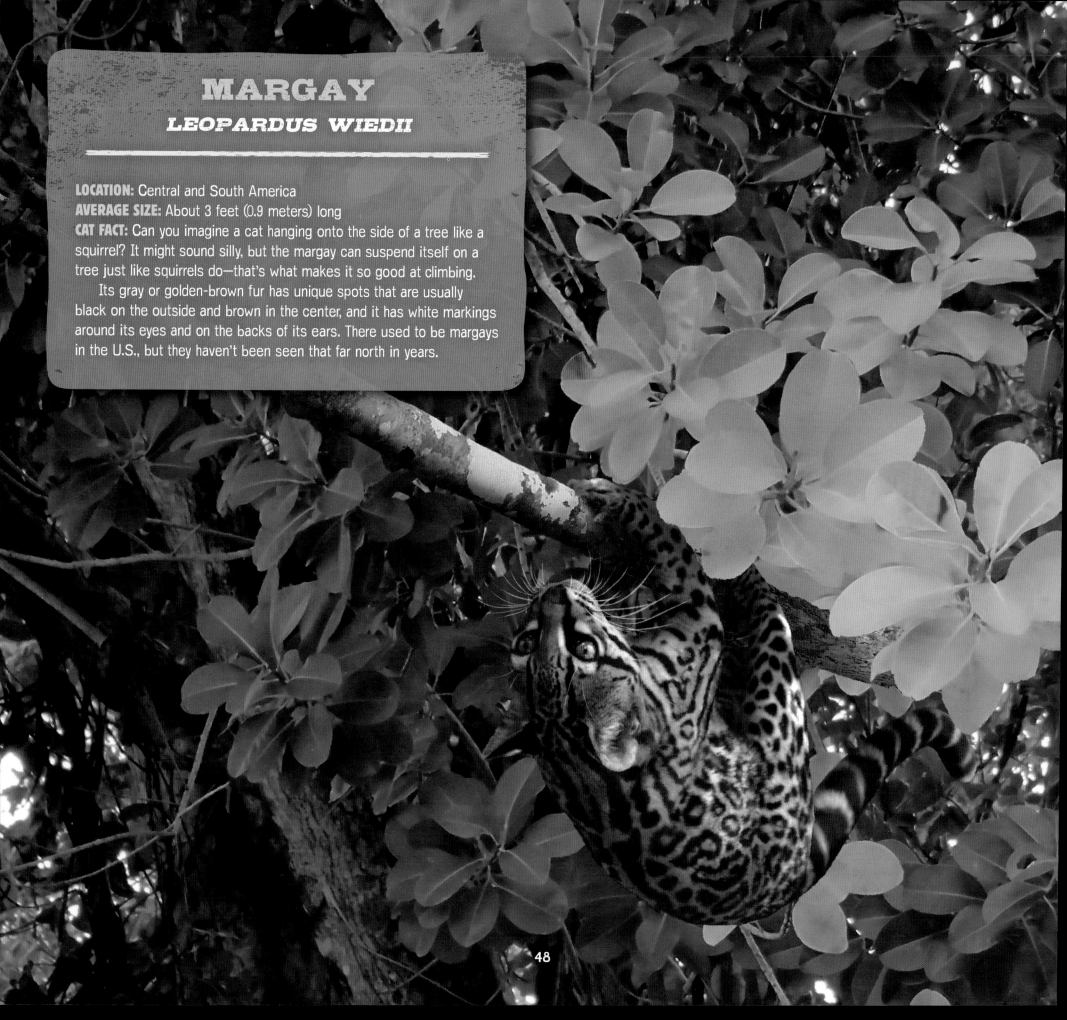

MARGAY
LEOPARDUS WIEDII

LOCATION: Central and South America
AVERAGE SIZE: About 3 feet (0.9 meters) long
CAT FACT: Can you imagine a cat hanging onto the side of a tree like a squirrel? It might sound silly, but the margay can suspend itself on a tree just like squirrels do—that's what makes it so good at climbing.

Its gray or golden-brown fur has unique spots that are usually black on the outside and brown in the center, and it has white markings around its eyes and on the backs of its ears. There used to be margays in the U.S., but they haven't been seen that far north in years.

SUNDA CLOUDED LEOPARD
NEOFELIS DIARDI

LOCATION: Borneo and Sumatra

AVERAGE SIZE: About 3 feet (0.9 meters) long, plus a 3-foot-long tail

CAT FACT: You've probably looked up at the clouds and made out different animal shapes, but have you ever looked at an animal and seen clouds? The clouded leopard gets its name from the unique cloud-like pattern of rosettes on its body. The Sunda clouded leopard has smaller markings and grayer fur than the mainland clouded leopards. You can tell whether one of these leopards is male or female by looking at its tail. Males have long, slender tails, but females have tails that are fluffy.

There's plenty to hunt in the Sunda clouded leopard's hilly, mountainous habitat, including monkeys, porcupines, pigs, deer, livestock, and fish. In Borneo, it has even been known to hunt orangutans.

MAINLAND CLOUDED LEOPARD
NEOFELIS NEBULOSA

LOCATION: Southeast Asia

AVERAGE SIZE: About 3 feet (0.9 meters) long, plus a 3-foot-long tail

CAT FACT: Clouded leopards have very long tails, but there's a practical reason for it. The mainland clouded leopard lives in tropical forests, and its tail helps this tree-climbing cat to balance while it's high up on branches.

Like the Sunda clouded leopard, the mainland clouded leopard gets its name from the cloud-like markings on its yellowish fur. It has rings on its tail and a recognizable pink nose with black spots.

JAGUAR
PANTHERA ONCA

LOCATION: North and Central America

AVERAGE SIZE: About 4 to 6 feet (1.2 to 1.8 meters) long, plus a 2-foot-long tail (0.6 meters)

CAT FACT: Imagine taking on a crocodile—there aren't many predators fierce enough to try, except the jaguar! North and Central American jaguars prefer to hunt capybara and pig-like mammals called peccaries, but they'll also take down deer and caimans (a South American crocodilian reptile) if they're available. The Central American jaguars live in thick forests and are about half the size of those in South America.

Jaguars are grouped in with lions and tigers as roaring cats. Jaguars are actually the only roaring cats that live in the western hemisphere. This orange cat with black spots doesn't just roar; it also snarls, growls, and grunts.

AFRICAN FOREST LEOPARD
PANTHERA PARDUS PARDUS

LOCATION: Africa

AVERAGE SIZE: 5 to 7 feet (1.5 to 2.1 meters) long

CAT FACT: Have you ever heard stories about cats getting stuck in trees? Well, these cats are up in the trees, but they're definitely not stuck! Leopards in the forests of Africa love climbing trees, and they can easily move from branch to branch. They'll stay up there to eat, nap, relax, and watch other animals. But when they come down, look out—they jump down headfirst! The forest leopard has great balance, and it always lands on its feet.

Forest leopards are actually the same species as African savanna leopards (see page 41), but their coats are a little darker. They're more of a reddish-orange to better blend with their forest home. The leopards behave differently based on their environment.

MARBLED CAT
PARDOFELIS MARMORATA MARMORATA

LOCATION: Southeast Asia and the Eastern Himalayas

AVERAGE SIZE: About 2 feet (0.6 meters) long

CAT FACT: The word marbled might have you thinking about stone, not fur. The marbled cat has gray fur and large blotches that merge together in a marble pattern. Marbled cats are good climbers thanks to their retractable claws and bushy tails. Their claws can grip onto bark, and their tails help them balance. *Pardofelis marmorata marmorata* can be found from the Malay Peninsula to Sumatra and Borneo.

AMUR LEOPARD CAT
PRIONAILURUS BENGALENSIS EUPTILURA

LOCATION: Northern Asia

AVERAGE SIZE: About 2 feet (0.6 meters) long

CAT FACT: This type of leopard cat can be found in the area near the Amur River, but its color varies depending on where it lives. In southern populations, its fur is typically yellowish in color, but in northern populations it's silvery gray.

The Amur leopard cat has a dark stripe across its cheeks and reddish-brown spots that are subtler than the markings on other types of leopard cats.

CHAPTER 4

COLD CATS: HILLS & SNOW

When it gets cold in the winter you might reach for a jacket, but cats have a built-in jacket of their own. Their soft fur can keep them warm in frigid environments, from snowy mountain ranges to hilly, freezing forests. These cold-weather cats are crafty, and they know that surviving in the chill is no easy feat. In this chapter, we'll look at how cats have adapted to live in harsh environments, from having a lighter color to blend in with the snow to having extra fur or hiding in dens for protection.

KODKOD
LEOPARDUS GUIGNA

LOCATION: South America
AVERAGE SIZE: About 1.5 feet (0.45 meters) long
CAT FACT: How can a small cat survey the forest easily? From the tops of trees! The kodkod, also known as the guigna, is an excellent climber, which serves two purposes. High ground is a great lookout point for the kodkod to search for prey (it especially likes rodents, reptiles, birds, and large insects). The second purpose is to hide. When predators come after the kodkod it quickly climbs up into the trees to escape.

The kodkod has yellowish or grayish fur with dark spots that sometimes streak down its back, and its thick tail has rings on it.

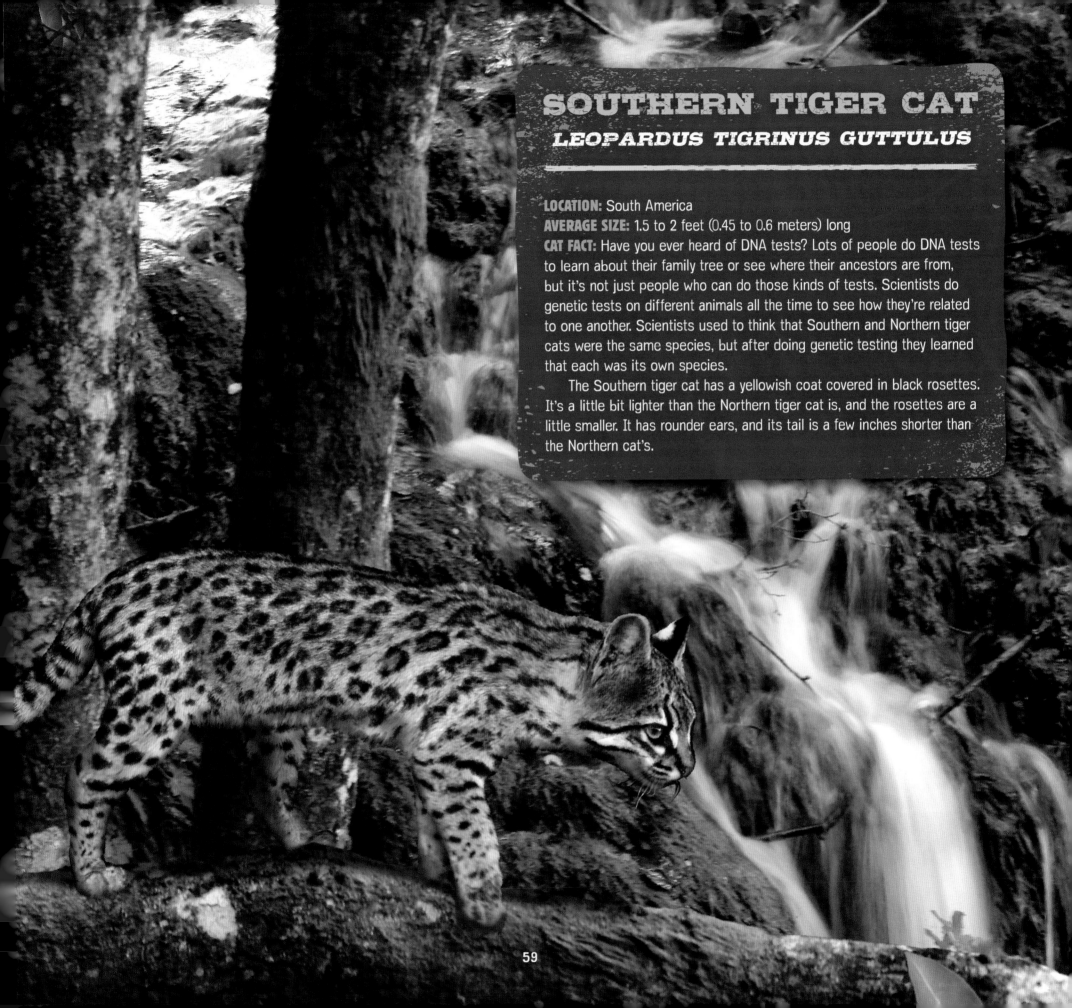

SOUTHERN TIGER CAT
LEOPARDUS TIGRINUS GUTTULUS

LOCATION: South America
AVERAGE SIZE: 1.5 to 2 feet (0.45 to 0.6 meters) long
CAT FACT: Have you ever heard of DNA tests? Lots of people do DNA tests to learn about their family tree or see where their ancestors are from, but it's not just people who can do those kinds of tests. Scientists do genetic tests on different animals all the time to see how they're related to one another. Scientists used to think that Southern and Northern tiger cats were the same species, but after doing genetic testing they learned that each was its own species.

The Southern tiger cat has a yellowish coat covered in black rosettes. It's a little bit lighter than the Northern tiger cat is, and the rosettes are a little smaller. It has rounder ears, and its tail is a few inches shorter than the Northern cat's.

NORTHERN TIGER CAT
LEOPARDUS TIGRINUS

LOCATION: Central America
AVERAGE SIZE: 1.5 to 2 feet (0.45 to 0.6 meters) long
CAT FACT: Picture an angry house cat that's spitting, hissing, arching its back, and showing its teeth. When the Northern tiger cat is angry it does all the same defensive moves to scare off the threat. The Northern tiger cat lives in a wide range of habitats, sometimes close to humans. It can be found in forests, tropical areas, savannas, scrubs, and wet, swampy areas. It is a great climber, but it spends most of its time on the ground hunting prey.

CANADA LYNX
LYNX CANADENSIS

LOCATION: North America
AVERAGE SIZE: 3 to 4 feet (0.9 to 1.2 meters) long
CAT FACT: In the snowy forests of Canada and the northern U.S., the lynx prowls, looking for snowshoe hares. It's not easy to walk through the snow, but the Canada lynx has fully retractable claws and powerful hind legs that make it less challenging. They aren't the only predators out there; wolves and mountain lions hunt in the same areas, and if the lynx isn't careful it could easily become their prey. Its yellow-brown to silvery-gray fur gives it some camouflage, but for young lynx it's important to stay out of harm's way. Mothers will give birth in dens made of things like fallen logs, stumps, or piles of branches and woody debris.

Lynx have trademark tufted ears and stubby tails that make them easy to identify in comparison to other cats.

EURASIAN LYNX
LYNX LYNX

LOCATION: Europe and Asia

AVERAGE SIZE: About 4 feet (1.2 meters) long

CAT FACT: The Eurasian lynx has a pawprint that's three times the size of a house cat's; it measures at three inches wide. The Eurasian lynx is the largest of the lynx species, and it has the tufted ears and stubby tail that all lynx share. It was once thought to be extinct in certain areas, but there have been some successful resettling efforts to bring it back.

This cat likes leftovers. The Eurasian lynx hunts prey like deer and reindeer, but since the prey is so large it will sometimes leave it and return for a few nights to finish its meal.

PALLAS'S CAT
OTOCOLOBUS MANUL

LOCATION: Asia

AVERAGE SIZE: 2 feet (0.6 meters) long

CAT FACT: Have you ever seen a cat's eyes turn into slits? Most cats have pupils that turn into slits when they get smaller, but not Pallas's cat. When the pupils in their owl-like yellow eyes get smaller, they stay circular. With the cold winds and dust storms common to their chilly environment, their eyes need a little extra protection. They have a unique third eyelid to protect their eyes from anything getting in.

They live near the Caucasus Mountains, so they need to stay warm. Their bellies have thick, soft, fluffy fur that's twice as long as the fur on their backs.

ARABIAN LEOPARD
PANTHERA PARDUS NIMR

LOCATION: Arabian Peninsula

AVERAGE SIZE: 6 to 7 feet (1.8 to 2.1 meters) long

CAT FACT: There are only a few Arabian leopards left in the mountainous region of the Arabian Peninsula. Today there are fewer than 200 of this critically endangered cat, which is the smallest of the leopard subspecies. The area where it lives is a harsh environment, and it competes with the caracal and the Arabian wolf for food—rodents, hare, hedgehogs, porcupines, and gazelles—and resources.

SNOW LEOPARD
PANTHERA UNCIA

LOCATION: Central and South Asia

AVERAGE SIZE: 4 to 5 feet (1.2 to 1.5 meters) long, plus a 3-foot-long tail

CAT FACT: Someone get this cat a blanket! The snow leopard lives in freezing, snowy areas, but it has some extra protection. It uses its long tail to cover its feet and face so it doesn't get too cold, and it molts its coat twice a year so that it has thicker fur in the winter.

The snow leopard has been called the "mountain ghost" because it's so rarely seen. It has a gray body and grayish rosettes that help it blend into the snowy, rocky terrain. It likes to use those rocks to hide so it can ambush its prey from above, and it has powerful hind legs that allow it to easily jump down. During the day it sometimes rests on cliffs, and it would rather stay high up in the mountains—as far up as 16,400 feet (5,000 meters)—than come down to the forest below.

CHAPTER 5

CATS WITH WET FEET

You may have heard that cats don't like water, and for some house cats that's definitely true. But in the wild there are lots of cats that not only live near the water, but love being in it! In this chapter, we'll look at cats that can swim and dive, that play in the water, and that live in some of the wettest areas in the world.

JAGUAR
PANTHERA ONCA

LOCATION: South America

AVERAGE SIZE: 4 to 6 feet (1.2 to 1.8 meters) long, plus a 2-foot-long tail (0.6 meters)

CAT FACT: In Brazil, there's a wetland area called the Pantanal region where cattle ranchers bring their herds to graze during the rainy season. For the jaguar, that's basically a meal handed right to them. The jaguar's broad feet and stubby, spread-out toes help it navigate the muddy ground, so it hunts both on land and in the water for prey like livestock, capybaras, peccaries, and caimans.

The Brazilian Pantanal form of the jaguar has a distinct rosette pattern on its orangey fur, including a row of spots down its back that can sometimes merge into a stripe. The populations of jaguars living in South America are larger than those living in Central America. Central American forms have smaller bodies that help them maneuver in thick forest habitats, while Pantanal jaguars live in more open habitats and have evolved to be larger as a result.

SUNDA LEOPARD CAT

PRIONAILURUS JAVANENSIS

LOCATION: Southeast Asia

AVERAGE SIZE: About 1.5 feet (0.45 meters) long

CAT FACT: The Sunda leopard cat is one of the few cats that has adapted to living in island habitats, and it can be found in areas like lowlands and plantations. In Java, the Sunda leopard cat will even explore rice paddies sometimes. But this habitat can also be dangerous. The Sunda leopard cat is hunted by the reticulated python, which is the world's longest snake!

Like other leopard cats, the Sunda leopard cat has small spots on its orangey fur, plus bands along its head and white markings around its eyes.

FLAT-HEADED CAT
PRIONAILURUS PLANICEPS

LOCATION: Malaysia, Southern Thailand, Sumatra, and Borneo

AVERAGE SIZE: About 1.5 feet (0.45 meters) long

CAT FACT: Who doesn't love seafood? The flat-headed cat's main diet comes from shallow freshwater and includes fish, frogs, shrimp, and aquatic fauna. It washes its food clean in the water and then brings it to the shore to eat. The flat-headed cat's claws don't fully retract, and it has webbing between its toes, which helps it walk better on the muddy ground. The claws don't always touch the ground, but they're always visible.

Its name comes from its flat forehead, and its eyes are especially close together, helping it see and catch prey in the water.

FISHING CAT
PRIONAILURUS VIVERRINUS

LOCATION: South and Southeast Asia

AVERAGE SIZE: About 3 feet (0.9 meters) long

CAT FACT: When scuba divers go into cold water, they wear wet suits to keep themselves warm. The fishing cat has its own built-in wet suit. The dense, compact layer of fur right by its skin has tightly packed hair that keeps water off its skin and keeps it warm, and the longer hairs that stick out on top give the fur a unique texture and pattern that works as camouflage—these are called guard hairs.

The fishing cat doesn't need a hook and line to catch its dinner. It uses its claws to scoop fish right out of the deep water, and it can swim long distances and dive under the surface very well. It loves being in the water, and scientists have even spotted it playing in shallow areas.

CHAPTER 6

VERSATILE GENERALISTS

Cats are smart and adaptable animals, and there are some species of cats that can thrive almost anywhere. In this chapter we're talking about the cats that are abundant in nature, from cougars that roam huge ranges in North and South America to bobcats that can live just about anywhere. You'll find these cats in wild places all over the world.

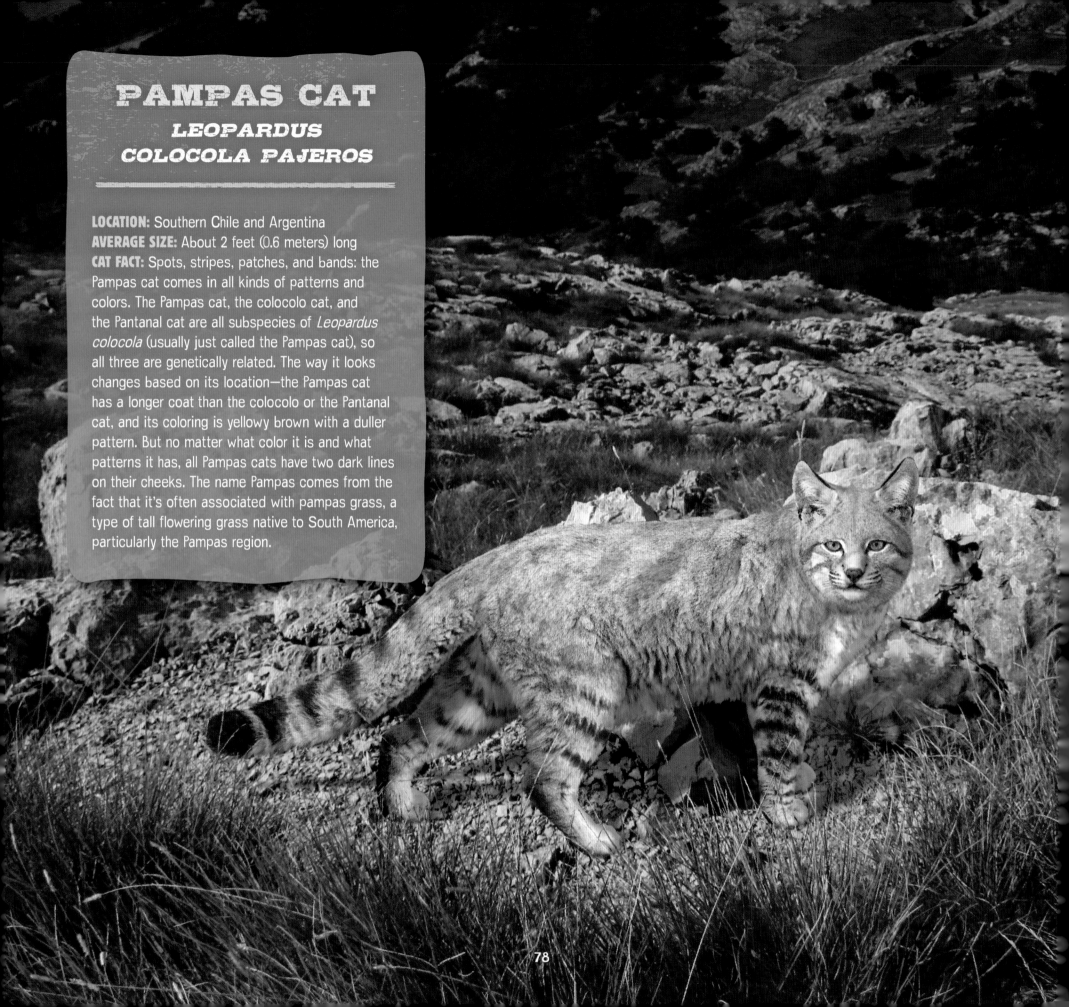

PAMPAS CAT
LEOPARDUS
COLOCOLA PAJEROS

LOCATION: Southern Chile and Argentina
AVERAGE SIZE: About 2 feet (0.6 meters) long
CAT FACT: Spots, stripes, patches, and bands: the Pampas cat comes in all kinds of patterns and colors. The Pampas cat, the colocolo cat, and the Pantanal cat are all subspecies of *Leopardus colocola* (usually just called the Pampas cat), so all three are genetically related. The way it looks changes based on its location—the Pampas cat has a longer coat than the colocolo or the Pantanal cat, and its coloring is yellowy brown with a duller pattern. But no matter what color it is and what patterns it has, all Pampas cats have two dark lines on their cheeks. The name Pampas comes from the fact that it's often associated with pampas grass, a type of tall flowering grass native to South America, particularly the Pampas region.

COLOCOLO CAT
LEOPARDUS COLOCOLA COLOCOLA

LOCATION: Central Chile

AVERAGE SIZE: About 2 feet (0.6 meters) long

CAT FACT: The nose knows. The colocolo cat is often confused with the Andean mountain cat, but you can tell the difference between the two by looking at their noses. Andean mountain cats have black noses, but the colocolo has a pink nose. The colocolo has a gray or red body with reddish stripes and dark spots.

79

PANTANAL CAT
LEOPARDUS COLOCOLA BRACCATUS

LOCATION: Brazil and Paraguay
AVERAGE SIZE: About 2 feet (0.6 meters) long
CAT FACT: Hybridization happens when one species of cat breeds with another. Their kittens are hybrids, meaning they have traits from both species. That's what happens with the Pantanal cat and the Northern tiger cat. The two species sometimes hybridize since they live in the same area of Brazil. The Pantanal cat is rust-colored with black bands, and its name comes from its home near the Pantanal wetlands.

GEOFFROY'S CAT
LEOPARDUS GEOFFROYI

LOCATION: South America
AVERAGE SIZE: About 2 feet (0.6 meters) long, plus a 1-foot-long tail (0.3 meters)
CAT FACT: Domesticated cats that use litter boxes like to bury their feces, and you might think wild cats would do the same. But Geoffroy's cat doesn't bury its feces, and that's because it uses the scent to mark its location. It will come back to the same spot repeatedly, kind of like its own personal bathroom.

Geoffroy's cat is one of the most widespread cats in South America, and it sometimes interbreeds with the Southern tiger cat. In northern parts of South America it has an orangey color, but in southern areas it's paler and grayer with black spots and bands.

BOBCAT
LYNX RUFUS

LOCATION: North America
AVERAGE SIZE: Up to 4 feet (1.2 meters) long
CAT FACT: Imagine you were on a boat tour and you encountered a bobcat. You would probably be shocked, and maybe even a little scared. That's exactly what happened in 2018 when a bobcat snuck onto a tourist boat in downtown Pittsburgh, Pennsylvania. It must have really wanted to see the sights! Bobcats are super adaptable and can be found in most parts of the U.S., along with Canada and Mexico, and they live right on the edge of human settlements. That means that they are frequently spotted, and they sometimes get into sticky situations.

If you were talking about a human with a bob, you might be thinking of a short haircut. The bobcat doesn't have the same stylish 'do, but it does have a short (bobbed) tail that gives it the name, and it also has recognizably large, tufted ears.

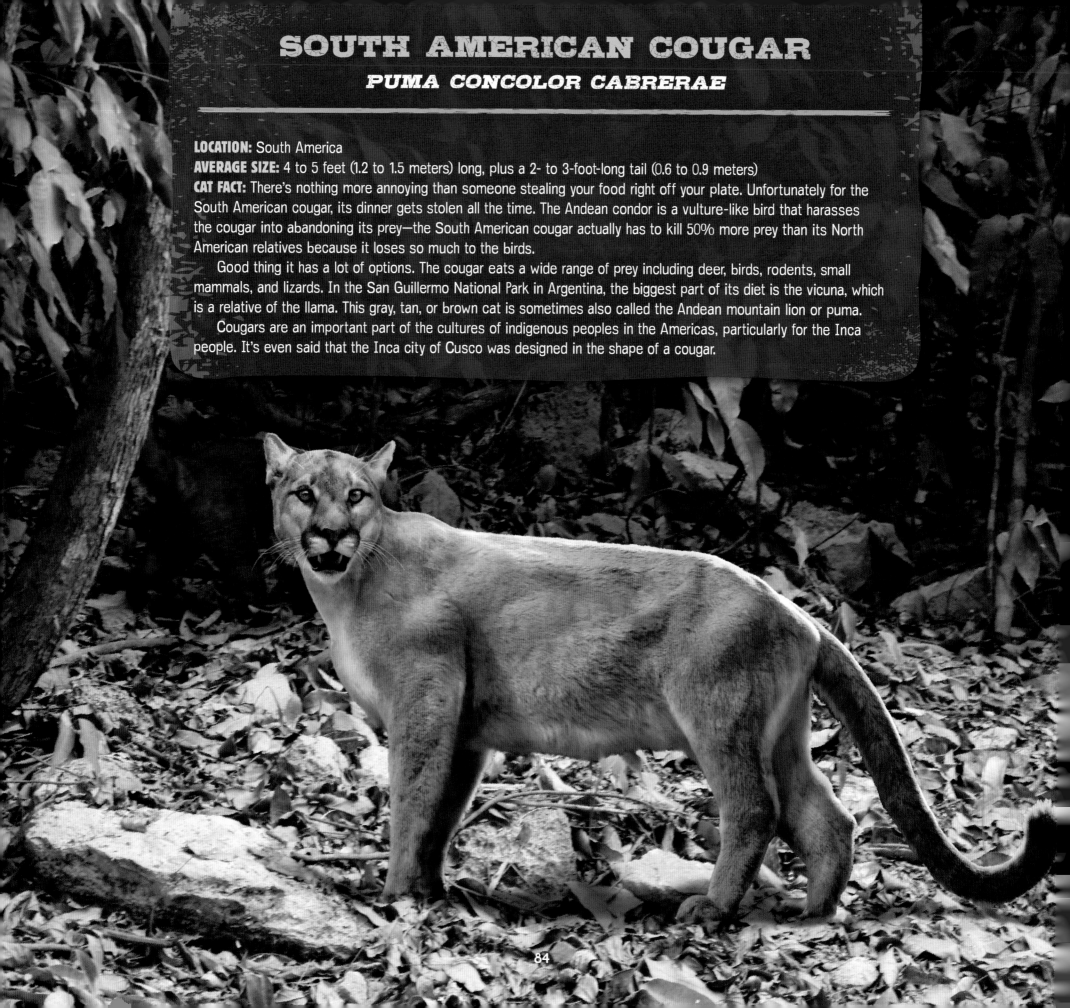

SOUTH AMERICAN COUGAR
PUMA CONCOLOR CABRERAE

LOCATION: South America

AVERAGE SIZE: 4 to 5 feet (1.2 to 1.5 meters) long, plus a 2- to 3-foot-long tail (0.6 to 0.9 meters)

CAT FACT: There's nothing more annoying than someone stealing your food right off your plate. Unfortunately for the South American cougar, its dinner gets stolen all the time. The Andean condor is a vulture-like bird that harasses the cougar into abandoning its prey—the South American cougar actually has to kill 50% more prey than its North American relatives because it loses so much to the birds.

Good thing it has a lot of options. The cougar eats a wide range of prey including deer, birds, rodents, small mammals, and lizards. In the San Guillermo National Park in Argentina, the biggest part of its diet is the vicuna, which is a relative of the llama. This gray, tan, or brown cat is sometimes also called the Andean mountain lion or puma.

Cougars are an important part of the cultures of indigenous peoples in the Americas, particularly for the Inca people. It's even said that the Inca city of Cusco was designed in the shape of a cougar.

NORTH AMERICAN COUGAR
PUMA CONCOLOR COUGUAR

LOCATION: Western North America

AVERAGE SIZE: 4 to 5 feet (1.2 to 1.5 meters) long, plus a 2- to 3-foot-long tail (0.6 to 0.9 meters)

CAT FACT: How many nicknames can you come up with for yourself? Probably not as many as the cougar. It's also called a puma, a panther, a mountain lion, and a whole bunch of other names. It even holds a Guinness World Record as the animal with the most nicknames. In English there are 40 different names for this type of cat.

The North American cougar used to be a lot more widespread, but it was declared extinct in the eastern part of the continent. This solid tan cat is still prominent in western Canada and the western U.S., and some nomadic ones venture into eastern areas. They were pushed out of the east because of settlers and habitat loss, but scientists think there's a possibility that they could resettle there. Their favorite prey is deer, but they have fierce competition with jaguars and bears living in the same areas.

CHAPTER 7

BLACK BEAUTIES

A cat's coloring is based on genetics, just like how the color of your hair, eyes, and skin is based on your genes. They inherit the genes from their parents, and what they look like is a result of those genes. But some cats have a trait called melanism that can make them look drastically different from other cats in the same species. Melanism is an increase of pigment in the skin or hair that causes the cat to be a much darker color. In this chapter, we're going to explore some of the most well-known examples of melanism.

KING CHEETAH
ACINONYX JUBATUS

LOCATION: Africa

AVERAGE SIZE: Around 4 to 5 feet (1.2 to 1.5 meters) long, plus a 2- to 3-foot-long tail (0.6 to 0.9 meters)

CAT FACT: This cheetah looks like it has racing stripes! Cheetahs are the fastest animals on earth, and they can reach speeds of over 60 miles per hour in three minutes. The king cheetah is just like other cheetahs, but it has a genetic mutation that causes the spots on its back to merge into 3 long stripes. They also have black stripes near their eyes that look a little like tears.

MELANISTIC ASIAN GOLDEN CAT
CATOPUMA TEMMINCKII

LOCATION: Southeast Asia, Northeast India, and Southern China
AVERAGE SIZE: About 4 to 5 feet (1.2 to 1.5 meters) long
CAT FACT: The name "golden" is a little ironic in this case; this dark beauty is actually just a darker genetic mutation of the Asian golden cat, which does typically have golden fur. The first photo of a melanistic golden cat was taken in 2009, and they've been photographed in a few different locations since then, so it doesn't seem to be too uncommon for this cat to be melanistic.

MELANISTIC KODKOD
LEOPARDUS GUIGNA

LOCATION: Chile and Argentina
AVERAGE SIZE: About 1.5 feet (0.45 meters) long
CAT FACT: Don't expect to see the kodkod out in the wild. This elusive cat does not like people. If there's nobody around it will be active both at night and during the day, but when humans are nearby they only come out at night. And with its dark color, the melanistic kodkod would be difficult to spot.

Do you believe in vampires? Near where the kodkod lives, a lot of poultry turned up with two marks on their necks that looked an awful lot like vampire bites, and the locals started to suspect it was the work of bloodsuckers. It turned out to just be bite marks from the kodkod's canines, and it's not likely that they actually suck blood, but since these cats are so secretive, who knows…maybe the kodkod really is a vampire.

MELANISTIC SERVAL
LEPTAILURUS SERVAL

LOCATION: Africa

AVERAGE SIZE: About 2 feet (0.6 meters) long

CAT FACT: Have you ever heard that wearing black attracts the sun's heat more than lighter colors of clothing? That's because the black fabric absorbs more light, which gets converted into heat, which means you'll be warmer than you would in a lighter color. Melanistic servals are more common in the Aberdare Mountain Range of Kenya, and that adaptation may be for the same reason. The darker color helps them retain heat in their cold environment. Melanistic servals exist in non-mountainous areas, too, since the coloring is a genetic mutation.

BLACK JAGUAR
PANTHERA ONCA

LOCATION: Central and South America
AVERAGE SIZE: 4 to 6 feet (1.2 to 1.8 meters) long, plus a 2-foot-long tail (0.6 meters)
CAT FACT: If you like the superhero Black Panther, you might be wondering what, exactly, a black panther is. Black panthers aren't one type of cat. The name panther is a catch-all phrase for big cats in the Panthera family, so it can refer to both black jaguars and black leopards.

Even though it looks like it's all black, melanistic jaguars still have that rosette pattern on their skin. It's just a little harder to see against the dark background. Melanistic jaguars are more active at night than yellow jaguars.

MELANISTIC JUNGLE CAT
FELIS CHAUS

LOCATION: Europe, Asia, and the Nile River Valley of Africa
AVERAGE SIZE: About 2 feet (0.6 meters) long
CAT FACT: Jungle cats are sometimes called swamp cats because they live in wetland areas. They're great swimmers because of it, and can dive to catch fish, although they also eat rodents and birds. Their fur is dark-tipped, which makes them look speckled, and they can be varying shades of brown, red, yellow, or gray with a lighter belly and throat.

BLACK LEOPARD

PANTHERA PARDUS

LOCATION: Asia and Africa

AVERAGE SIZE: 5 to 7 feet (1.5 to 2.1 meters) long

CAT FACT: Like black jaguars, black leopards are sometimes called panthers. The black coloring is just a recessive gene in leopards that makes their pigment darker. The spots that leopards have are still there, but they're hard to see. Melanistic leopards are most often found in humid forests, and they're more common in East Asia than in other areas where leopards live. In southern Thailand and the Malaysian Peninsula the melanistic trait is so common that nearly all the leopards are black.

CHAPTER 8

THE MAKING OF THE CAT

Cats have been around for thousands of years, so how did we end up keeping them as house pets? The domesticated cat has been bred over time to evolve from its wild state to live with humans. It's not a bad thing for domesticated cats since they get shelter, food, and social interaction, and there's evidence that cats have been living with humans for thousands of years.

In the wild, there are some species of cats that aren't domesticated, but look and act a lot like the cats that are. They have similar traits and characteristics, and sometimes they'll even live near and interact with domesticated cats. In this chapter, we're looking at how the domestic cats you know and love came to be and some of the wild cats that are similar to them.

MAINLAND LEOPARD CAT
PRIONAILURUS BENGALENSIS

LOCATION: Asia

AVERAGE SIZE: 1.5 to 2 feet (0.45 to 0.6 meters) long

CAT FACT: In central China, scientists found 5,000-year-old fossils that indicated the ancient people had domesticated leopard cats. Other types of cats became more popular domestic choices after that. Nowadays, leopard cats are the most widespread felines in Asia, and they're wild cats. But even though true leopard cats aren't domesticated, they have very close domesticated relatives. The Bengal cat is a crossbreed that's part domesticated cat and part leopard cat!

98

SAND CAT
FELIS MARGARITA

LOCATION: Asia and Africa
AVERAGE SIZE: About 1.5 feet long (0.45 meters)
CAT FACT: That fluffy face may make the sand cat look snuggly, but don't be fooled by its teddy bear appearance. Its prey includes the venomous sand viper, along with other reptiles, rodents, and birds. Its sandy color helps it blend into the deserts where it lives, and it has a lot of adaptations to be able to survive in such a harsh environment.

Sand cats have wiry, dense fur that grows between their toes and helps them in the drastic temperatures of the desert. In the day, temperatures can hit 120 degrees Fahrenheit, but at night they can fall to freezing temperatures of about 20 degrees Fahrenheit, so the fur protects its paws in these extremes. During the day, the cat burrows down into the sand to escape the worst of the heat, coming out at dusk as it cools off.

Its fluffy inner ears keep sand from blowing in during windy sandstorms, and it gets its hydration from its prey, so it doesn't need to rely on a source of water to live.

JUNGLE CAT
FELIS CHAUS

LOCATION: Europe, Asia, and the Nile River Valley of Africa
AVERAGE SIZE: About 2 feet (0.6 meters) long
CAT FACT: If your house had a problem with mice, you would want to have a jungle cat around. Its main diet is small rodents, and it eats 3 to 5 a day. Jungle cats also eat birds and fish, and in southern Russia they even eat olives.

The jungle cat has recognizable bright yellow eyes and dark stripes at the top of its legs. In southern populations, the stripes are lighter than in northern ones.

CHINESE MOUNTAIN CAT
FELIS BIETI

LOCATION: Western China
AVERAGE SIZE: About 2.5 feet (0.75 meters) long
CAT FACT: Mama mountain cats have to be very cautious to keep their young away from bears and wolves in the mountains. Mothers keep their young buried in burrows so they're protected until they're large enough to venture out.

You might have guessed from the name that mountain cats live in the mountains, and they have a dense layer of fur to keep them warm in the chilly environment. Their sandy fur has faint markings on the face and legs, plus bands on the short, bushy, black-tipped tail. Mountain cats were formerly considered to be a type of wildcat, but they have since been separated into their own species.

EUROPEAN WILDCAT
FELIS SILVESTRIS

LOCATION: Europe

AVERAGE SIZE: About 2 feet (0.6 meters) long

CAT FACT: You might be thinking these wildcats look an awful lot like the pets you'd see in a home, and that's because they're very closely related. Wildcats live in areas very close to humans, and they'll interact and breed with domesticated cats. That might sound like a good thing, but it can cause some problems. Wildcats can catch diseases from domesticated cats, and they have to compete with feral domestic cats for rodents. Being close to humans also means that traffic accidents are a threat, and wildcats can get sick or die from rodent poisons that people use to get rid of pests. The crossbreeding with domestic cats also means that there are fewer and fewer true wildcats, which means that the genes of the species could eventually get wiped out. Wildcats used to be a lot more common, but they've gone regionally extinct in some countries because of a combination of human interaction and habitat loss.

SOUTHERN AFRICAN WILDCAT
FELIS LYBICA CAFRA

LOCATION: Southern and Eastern Africa

AVERAGE SIZE: About 2 feet (0.6 meters) long

CAT FACT: Wildcats living near human settlements have easy access to livestock like lamb and poultry as a food source. But the owners of that livestock are never thrilled to find that their animals have been killed by a wildcat. In some areas, wildcats are considered pests because of the problems they cause with livestock.

Southern African wildcats look very similar to African wildcats with their reddish fur and faint, tabby-like markings, but genetic testing has shown that they are two separate species.

ASIATIC WILDCAT

FELIS LYBICA ORNATA

LOCATION: Southwest and Central Asia

AVERAGE SIZE: About 2 feet (0.6 meters) long

CAT FACT: Cats aren't born with all the skills they need to hunt; they have to learn them. Wildcats learn how to hunt from their mothers, who have their young practice with easy-to-catch prey like injured animals, insects, or bird eggs.

In central Asia, the wildcats are gray, yellow, or reddish in color, but in other areas they're sandy-colored. They often have spots and a long, black-tipped tail.

AFRICAN WILDCAT
FELIS LYBICA LYBICA

LOCATION: Eastern, Western, and North Africa

AVERAGE SIZE: About 2 feet (0.6 meters) long

CAT FACT: All domesticated cats diverged from wild cats about 9,000 years ago, from a species called *Felis silvestris lybica*. That species came from an area called the Fertile Crescent between Asia and Africa, near where African wildcats now live.

The wildcat looks a lot like a big tabby cat, and it likes the same kind of prey domesticated cats do, including rodents, birds, lizards, frogs, and fish. Living near humans can be a big advantage for wildcats. Where people are, there are usually lots of rats and mice ready to scrounge through their trash—and wildcats love hunting rats and mice.

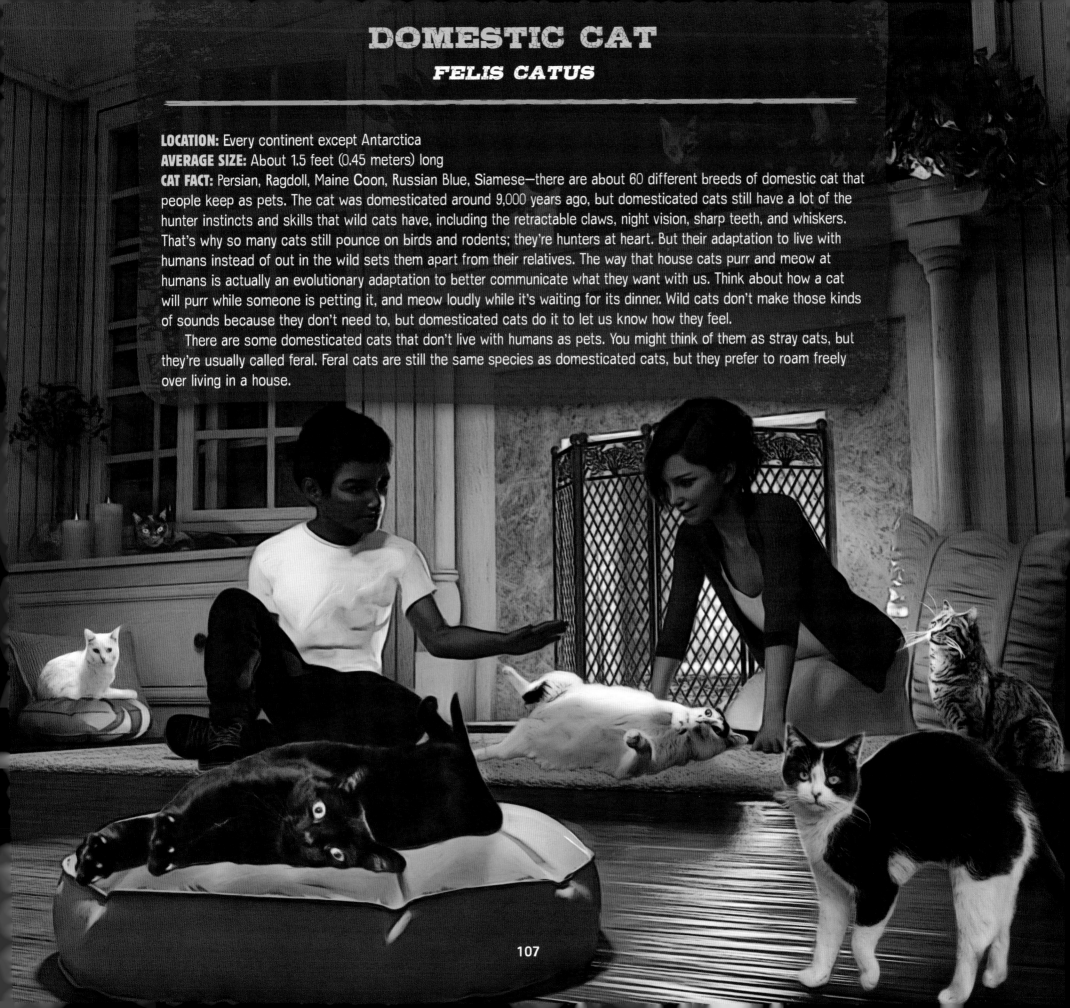

DOMESTIC CAT
FELIS CATUS

LOCATION: Every continent except Antarctica

AVERAGE SIZE: About 1.5 feet (0.45 meters) long

CAT FACT: Persian, Ragdoll, Maine Coon, Russian Blue, Siamese—there are about 60 different breeds of domestic cat that people keep as pets. The cat was domesticated around 9,000 years ago, but domesticated cats still have a lot of the hunter instincts and skills that wild cats have, including the retractable claws, night vision, sharp teeth, and whiskers. That's why so many cats still pounce on birds and rodents; they're hunters at heart. But their adaptation to live with humans instead of out in the wild sets them apart from their relatives. The way that house cats purr and meow at humans is actually an evolutionary adaptation to better communicate what they want with us. Think about how a cat will purr while someone is petting it, and meow loudly while it's waiting for its dinner. Wild cats don't make those kinds of sounds because they don't need to, but domesticated cats do it to let us know how they feel.

There are some domesticated cats that don't live with humans as pets. You might think of them as stray cats, but they're usually called feral. Feral cats are still the same species as domesticated cats, but they prefer to roam freely over living in a house.

CHAPTER 9

SUPERLATIVES

Cats come in all different shapes, sizes, and colors. In this chapter, we're going to look at the cats that are the absolute best of the best at what they do—the unique cats that stand out from the rest. We'll cover every size, from the tiniest rusty-spotted cat to the biggest tiger. Plus, we'll look at the quirkiest, most exciting cats like the social lion, the superfast cheetah, and the deadly black-footed cat.

CHEETAH
ACINONYX JUBATUS

LOCATION: Iran and Africa

AVERAGE SIZE: 4 to 5 feet (1.2 to 1.5 meters) long

CAT FACT: Picture this: you're in a car riding down the highway when, all of a sudden, a huge cat runs up alongside you! Cheetahs can run at speeds over 60 miles per hour, so they could easily catch up to a car. And they aren't just the fastest cat. Cheetahs are the fastest of any type of animal in the world. Their slim, long legs help them move quickly, but you won't see them on any old road. They're only in some parts of Africa and a small part of Iran, although they used to be a lot more widespread. Scientists think that they are currently only found in about 9% of the area they historically existed in. They were pushed out of the other 91% of their historic homes because of human interactions, including habitat loss and overhunting.

Unlike lion prides where the females group together, the female cheetah usually travels solo. However, males will sometimes form groups called coalitions. The few members in the group are usually brothers from the same litter, but sometimes unrelated cheetahs will join in. The coalition of cheetahs will live together, hunt together, and even groom each other.

FASTEST CAT

BLACK-FOOTED CAT
FELIS NIGRIPES

LOCATION: Africa

AVERAGE SIZE: About 1.5 feet (0.45 meters) long

CAT FACT: You might not think this tiny cat looks like a killer, but it's actually the most successful hunter of all the cats. That's because it has a really high success rate—when a black-footed cat goes after prey, it succeeds 60% of the time. Not all cats are so lucky (or crafty) when it comes to killing. Lions are about 200 times the size of black-footed cats, but lions only succeed in killing their prey 20 to 25% of the time.

Black-footed cats don't mind waiting for their dinner. They'll stake out rodent burrows and wait patiently for their prey to come out before they pounce. Black-footed cats especially like rodents and birds, but this tawny, darkly marked cat will grab any small critter it can.

MOST WEASELLY CAT

JAGUARUNDI
HERPAILURUS YAGOUAROUNDI

LOCATION: Southern North America and South America

AVERAGE SIZE: About 2 feet (0.6 meters) long

CAT FACT: Have you ever seen a ferret or a weasel with a long, slinky body? That's kind of what the jaguarundi looks like. Its rusty brown or charcoal gray coat is a solid color, and it has a super elongated back on short legs. It slinks around on the ground when it hunts, but it can also climb and jump well. A lot of cats like to hunt alone, but the jaguarundi has sometimes been spotted in pairs, too. They can communicate with one another really well, and they have at least 13 different types of calls that can convey anything from a greeting to a warning signal.

SERVAL
LEPTAILURUS SERVAL

LOCATION: Africa

AVERAGE SIZE: About 2 feet (0.6 meters) long

CAT FACT: With its incredibly long legs and neck, the serval has sometimes been called a giraffe cat. The serval's lanky body has dark spots and stripes on it, and its head and neck aren't the only body parts with strange proportions. Compared to the size of its head, its ears are enormous!

But like the wolf in *Little Red Riding Hood* says...the better to hear you with, my dear! Servals have great hearing, and they use those big ears to listen for prey while they wait in the grass. Then, when their prey comes by, they jump out and snatch it. They can leap almost 10 feet straight up, and they'll snatch birds flying by right out of the air.

LANKIEST CAT

LION
PANTHERA LEO

MOST SOCIAL CAT

LOCATION: Africa

AVERAGE SIZE: 8 to 10 feet (2.4 to 3 meters) long

CAT FACT: If you've watched *The Lion King*, you've probably heard the term "pride." Lions live in groups called prides that can have up to 40 lions. The prides are mostly made up of females (sometimes a dozen in one pride) and their cubs, and each pride has up to 3 adult male lions that serve as the protectors. The females do most of the hunting, and the males keep the females and cubs safe from potential threats with their intimidating manes and super loud roars.

Lions recognize their friends just like people do, and when they want to greet another lion they know they'll rub their heads together with their tails looped in the air. They like to chat with each other, too. They use their roars to communicate, and sometimes they'll even roar in a chorus together—kind of like the lion version of karaoke!

TIGER
PANTHERA TIGRIS

LOCATION: Asia

AVERAGE SIZE: Over 10 feet (3 meters) long

CAT FACT: How much can you eat in one meal? The tiger definitely has you beat; it can eat up to 80 pounds of meat at once! That explains why they weigh over 600 pounds. The tigers in continental Asia are the biggest of all cats, but there are other smaller species of tigers in surrounding island areas, too. They use their huge size to their advantage when hunting. They prefer to eat a group of animals called ungulates, which are large, hooved mammals (think giraffes, deer, cattle, and other animals with hooves). Tigers can have bursts of speed, but they can run quickly for long distances, so they tend to seek out slower prey like the very old or very young and then use their body weight to slam into their prey and knock it off balance.

Tigers are some of the most recognizable big cats. They have long, dark, vertical stripes that help them stay camouflaged in long grass, and they're typically rusty brown or orange. There are genetic variations that cause tigers to be white, golden, and even black. Their coloring goes all the way down to the hair follicles, so even if a tiger were shaved you would still see its stripes. These big beasts are an endangered species—100 years ago there were as many as 100,000 wild tigers across Asia, but now there are less than 4,000 left.

BIGGEST CAT

RUSTY-SPOTTED CAT

PRIONAILURUS RUBIGINOSUS

SMALLEST CAT

LOCATION: India and Sri Lanka

AVERAGE SIZE: 14 to 19 inches (35.5 to 48 centimeters) long

CAT FACT: It's hard to imagine a 3-pound cat taking down birds and rodents. The rusty-spotted cat is hardly bigger than its prey! It tends to live near where humans are, because there are usually more small rodents available near human settlements. It will also eat birds, lizards, frogs, and insects.

The rusty-spotted cat is smaller than most breeds of domestic cats, sometimes even half the size, and it's not the only tiny cat in the wild. Black-footed cats and kodkods are only slightly bigger than the rusty-spotted cat.

CHAPTER 10

ENDANGERED CATS

There are lots of reasons why animals become endangered. Sometimes there are natural causes, like bigger animals preying on them, that make it dangerous for cats. But more often it's human interference that puts species in danger. Towns and cities built on land where big cats live destroy their homes, and when they have a smaller habitat they also have a smaller food source. Some cats are killed because they're considered a nuisance when they kill livestock like cattle, poultry, and lamb. Hunting big cats also used to be popular, and the fur of a big cat was very valuable.

Overhunting and habitat loss are the two biggest factors that put many of these cats in danger. Rules and regulations on hunting help protect the cats, and many of their homes have been turned into wildlife preserves to make sure that they have somewhere to live. Many zoos and sanctuaries have breeding programs, and sometimes there are resettlement efforts to reintroduce a species into an area where it was considered extinct.

CRITICALLY ENDANGERED

ASIATIC CHEETAH

ACINONYX JUBATUS VENATICUS

LOCATION: Iran

AVERAGE SIZE: 4 feet (1.2 meters) long

CAT FACT: Cheetah populations have dwindled everywhere, but the subspecies *Acinonyx jubatus venaticus* has been hit particularly hard. It used to be found in North Africa and India, but now it only exists in the eastern half of Iran, and there may be fewer than 100 Asiatic cheetahs left.

The Asiatic cheetah has a thinner coat and fewer spots than the African cheetah, and it has a collection of small black spots in lines on its head and neck. Its coat is fawn-colored to blend in well with the sandy, dry areas where it lives.

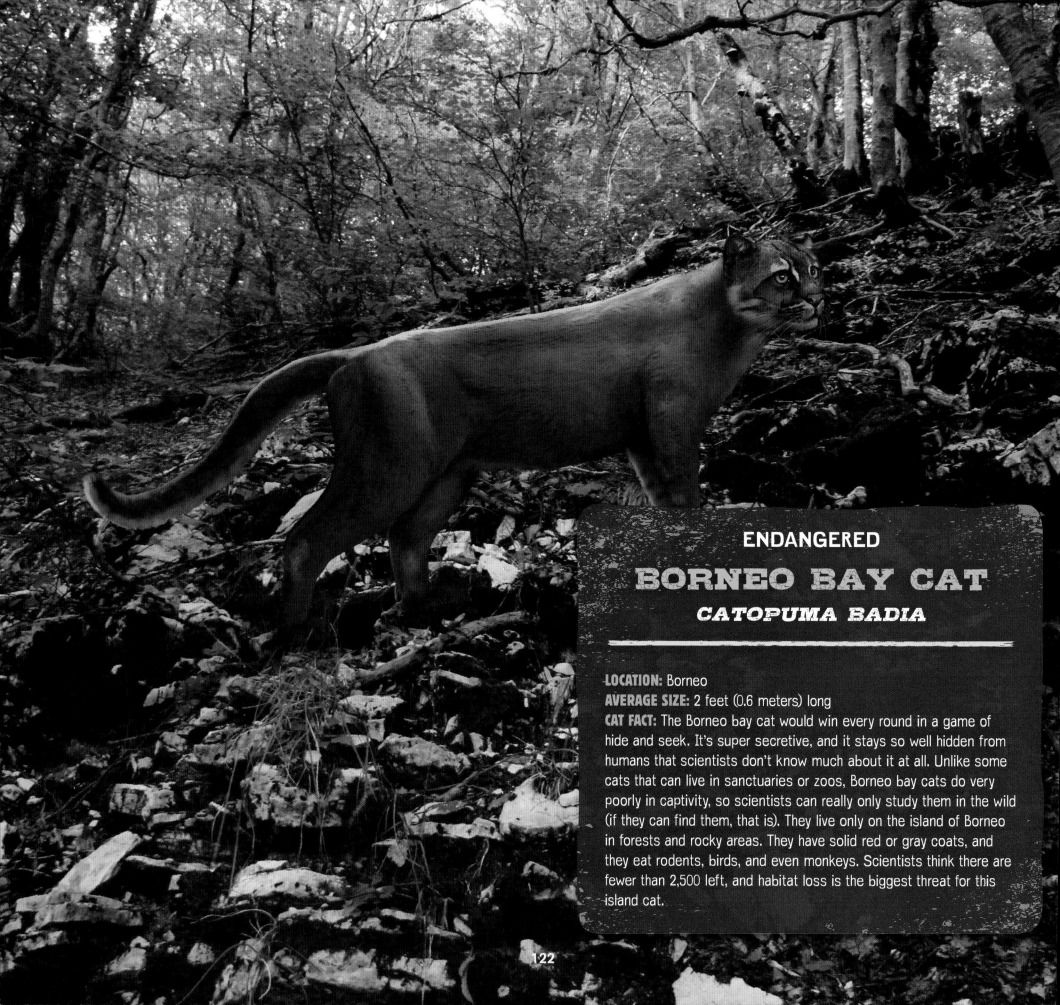

ENDANGERED

BORNEO BAY CAT
CATOPUMA BADIA

LOCATION: Borneo

AVERAGE SIZE: 2 feet (0.6 meters) long

CAT FACT: The Borneo bay cat would win every round in a game of hide and seek. It's super secretive, and it stays so well hidden from humans that scientists don't know much about it at all. Unlike some cats that can live in sanctuaries or zoos, Borneo bay cats do very poorly in captivity, so scientists can really only study them in the wild (if they can find them, that is). They live only on the island of Borneo in forests and rocky areas. They have solid red or gray coats, and they eat rodents, birds, and even monkeys. Scientists think there are fewer than 2,500 left, and habitat loss is the biggest threat for this island cat.

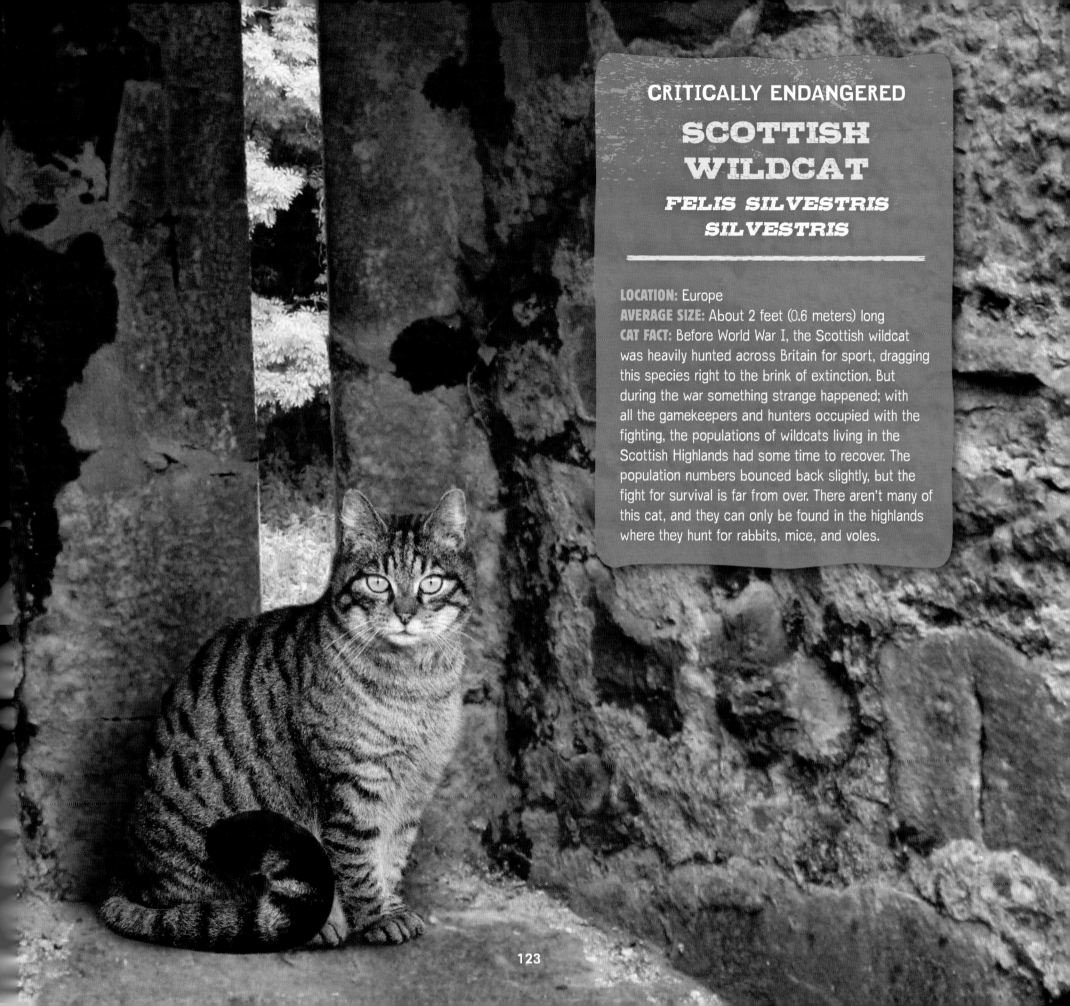

SCOTTISH WILDCAT
FELIS SILVESTRIS SILVESTRIS

LOCATION: Europe

AVERAGE SIZE: About 2 feet (0.6 meters) long

CAT FACT: Before World War I, the Scottish wildcat was heavily hunted across Britain for sport, dragging this species right to the brink of extinction. But during the war something strange happened; with all the gamekeepers and hunters occupied with the fighting, the populations of wildcats living in the Scottish Highlands had some time to recover. The population numbers bounced back slightly, but the fight for survival is far from over. There aren't many of this cat, and they can only be found in the highlands where they hunt for rabbits, mice, and voles.

123

ANDEAN MOUNTAIN CAT
LEOPARDUS JACOBITA

LOCATION: The Andes Mountains

AVERAGE SIZE: 2 feet (0.6 meters) long

CAT FACT: Are you a picky eater? The Andean mountain cat is. Its favorite things to eat are chinchillas and mountain viscachas, but those types of animals only live in certain areas of the Andes Mountains. So when the Andean mountain cat can't find them, it has to resort to eating other small mammals, birds, and lizards.

There are fewer than 2,500 Andean mountain cats left. This silvery gray cat with rust-colored spots looks like the colocolo cat, but you can tell the difference between the two by looking at their noses. The Andean mountain cat has a unique black nose and lips. Habitat loss is the biggest threat for this species, and it is sometimes hunted by farmers because it's known for killing livestock.

ENDANGERED

IBERIAN LYNX

LYNX PARDINUS

LOCATION: Iberian Peninsula and Southwestern Europe
AVERAGE SIZE: 3 to 4 feet (0.9 to 1.2 meters) long
CAT FACT: Can a cat have a beard? The Iberian lynx sure looks like it does. It has tufts on its ears and jaw that make it appear to have a long beard. If this cat looks old and wise to you, that's because it is. Fossils of the Iberian lynx date all the way back to the Pleistocene epoch.

It prefers to eat rabbits, but it will also eat ducks, birds, or young deer. Rabbits in the area where it lives were wiped out by many bouts of disease, so the Iberian lynx had to adapt. That strain on its food source mixed with habitat loss and hunting have put the Iberian lynx in danger.

ENDANGERED

ASIATIC LION

PANTHERA LEO LEO

LOCATION: India

AVERAGE SIZE: 7 to 8 feet (2.1 to 2.4 meters) long

CAT FACT: In the Gir Forest Reserve of India, there's a small population of a few hundred Asiatic lions. They're the only ones left of their kind. They're smaller than African lions, with shorter manes and larger tail tufts. The Gir Forest Reserve is a nature preserve, which means that their habitat is a safe place, and their numbers have grown slightly because of it in recent years.

Farmers will let their herds come to graze in the reserve, so cattle and goats make up a good part of the Asiatic lion's diet.

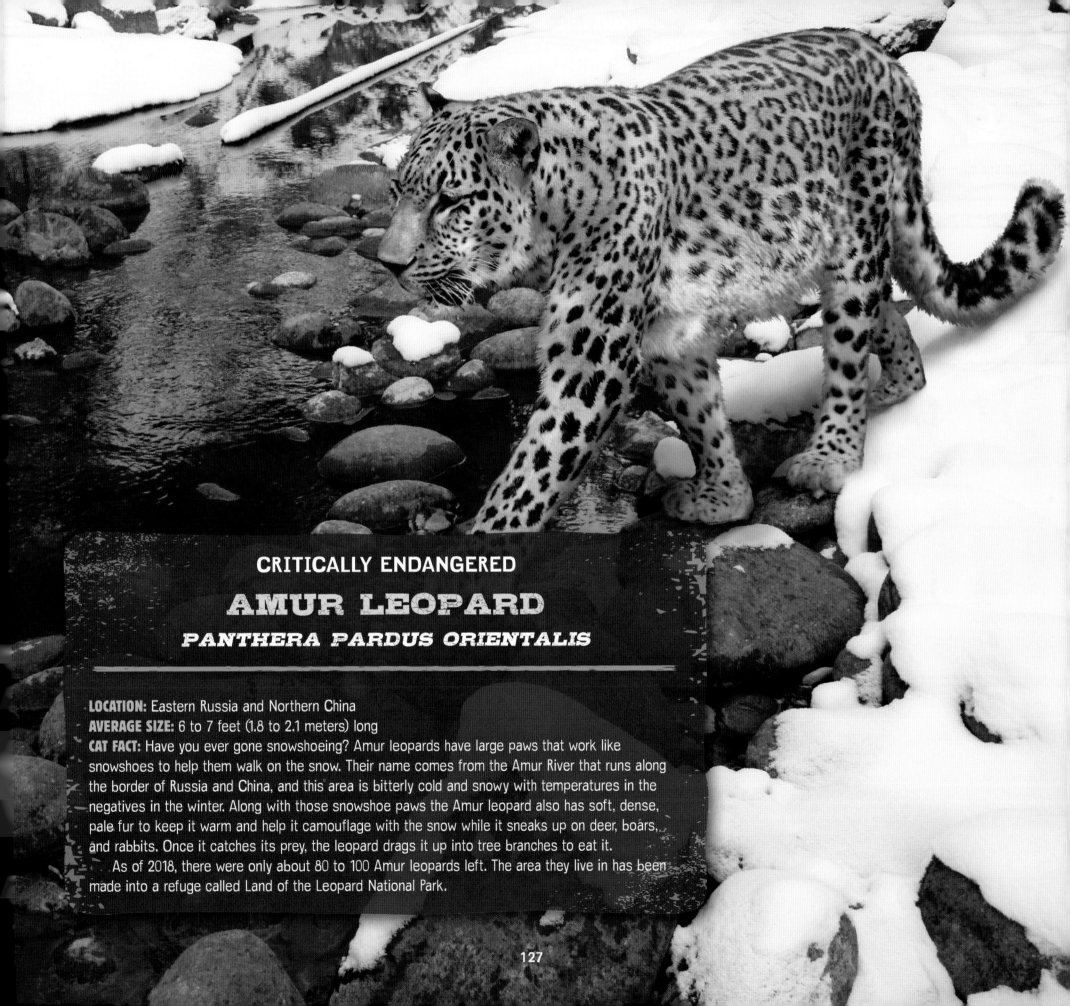

CRITICALLY ENDANGERED

AMUR LEOPARD
PANTHERA PARDUS ORIENTALIS

LOCATION: Eastern Russia and Northern China
AVERAGE SIZE: 6 to 7 feet (1.8 to 2.1 meters) long
CAT FACT: Have you ever gone snowshoeing? Amur leopards have large paws that work like snowshoes to help them walk on the snow. Their name comes from the Amur River that runs along the border of Russia and China, and this area is bitterly cold and snowy with temperatures in the negatives in the winter. Along with those snowshoe paws the Amur leopard also has soft, dense, pale fur to keep it warm and help it camouflage with the snow while it sneaks up on deer, boars, and rabbits. Once it catches its prey, the leopard drags it up into tree branches to eat it.

As of 2018, there were only about 80 to 100 Amur leopards left. The area they live in has been made into a refuge called Land of the Leopard National Park.

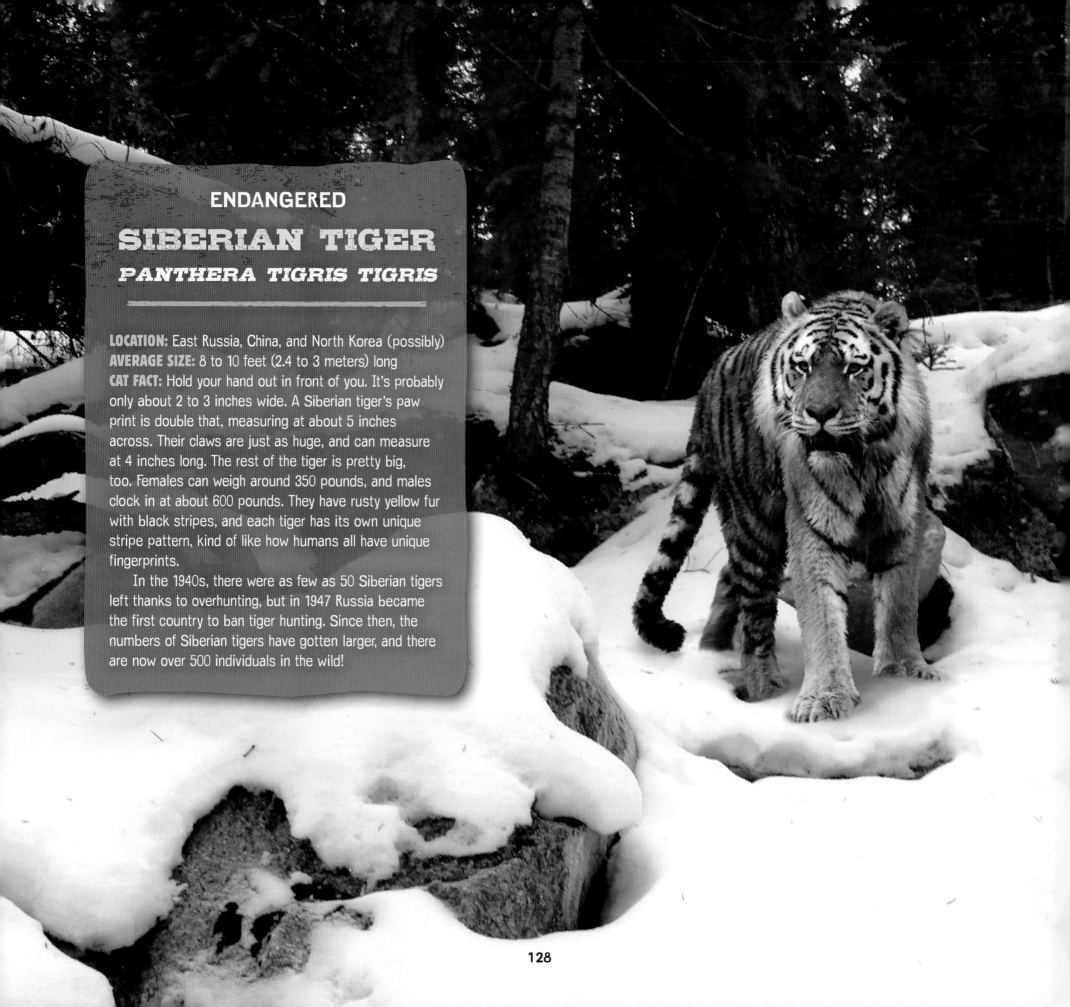

ENDANGERED

SIBERIAN TIGER
PANTHERA TIGRIS TIGRIS

LOCATION: East Russia, China, and North Korea (possibly)

AVERAGE SIZE: 8 to 10 feet (2.4 to 3 meters) long

CAT FACT: Hold your hand out in front of you. It's probably only about 2 to 3 inches wide. A Siberian tiger's paw print is double that, measuring at about 5 inches across. Their claws are just as huge, and can measure at 4 inches long. The rest of the tiger is pretty big, too. Females can weigh around 350 pounds, and males clock in at about 600 pounds. They have rusty yellow fur with black stripes, and each tiger has its own unique stripe pattern, kind of like how humans all have unique fingerprints.

In the 1940s, there were as few as 50 Siberian tigers left thanks to overhunting, but in 1947 Russia became the first country to ban tiger hunting. Since then, the numbers of Siberian tigers have gotten larger, and there are now over 500 individuals in the wild!

CRITICALLY ENDANGERED

IRIOMOTE ISLAND LEOPARD CAT

PRIONAILURUS BENGALENSIS IRIOMOTENSIS

LOCATION: Iriomote, Japan

AVERAGE SIZE: About 2 feet (0.6 meters) long

CAT FACT: Most cats stick to the mainland, but this leopard cat chose island life and lives only in one place: the island of Iriomote, Japan. That might sound like paradise, but it means that this cat has limited options for living space. As the areas where they dwell get more populated, they lose more of their habitats and encounter more danger from the people and their pets that live nearby. They're dusky brown and about the same size as domestic cats, so they can get caught up in fights with cats and dogs, competition for food like rodents, and even traffic accidents.

Part of the area where they live has been declared a protected wildlife area, and they can be found in hills and streams at dawn and dusk, climbing trees and swimming.

FLORIDA PANTHER
PUMA CONCOLOR CORYI

LOCATION: Southern Florida
AVERAGE SIZE: 6 to 7 feet (1.8 to 2.1 meters) long
CAT FACT: Imagine you're driving down the road and a panther jumps in your path. It might sound outrageous, but in Florida it's not unheard of, and these big cats have been known to cause accidents when they wander onto highways. You might have heard that cats don't like water, but that's not true of the Florida panther. It's a great swimmer that can easily cross swamps, and it lives in large wetland areas.

When Florida panthers are born they have blue eyes and spots, but as they age the spots fade into their tan coat and their eyes turn yellow. They have a whorl of hair in the middle of their backs, kind of like a cowlick. As of 2017, there were just over 200 in the wild.

INDEX

INDEX

INDEX

INDEX

About the Illustrator

Julius Csotonyi is one of the world's most high-profile and talented contemporary scientific illustrators. His considerable academic expertise informs his stunning, dynamic art. He has created life-sized dinosaur murals for the Royal Ontario Museum and for the Dinosaur Hall at the Natural History Museum of Los Angeles County, as well as most of the artwork for the exhibit "Deep Time" in the David H. Koch Hall of Fossils at the Smithsonian National Museum of Natural History in Washington, D.C. He lives in Canada.

His books include *Discovering Reptiles*, *Discovering Sharks*, *Discovering Bugs*, *The T. Rex Handbook*, *The Paleoart of Julius Csotonyi*, *Prehistoric Predators*, and *Dino World*.

About the Author

Kelly Gauthier is a Boston-based writer and editor.
When she's not working, she can often be found on a boat, in the water, or sitting on the end of a dock reading a book. She is also the author of *Discovering Reptiles*, *Discovering Whales*, *Discovering Planets and Moons*, *The Little Chunky Book of Dinosaurs*, and *The Little Chunky Book of Sharks*.

About Applesauce Press

Good ideas ripen with time. From seed to harvest, Applesauce Press creates books with beautiful designs, creative formats, and kid-friendly information. Like our parent company, Cider Mill Press Book Publishers, our press bears fruit twice a year, publishing a new crop of titles each spring and fall.

"Where Good Books Are Ready for Press"
Visit us online at
cidermillpress.com
or write to us at
12 Spring Street, PO Box 454
Kennebunkport, Maine 04046